Classroom, Laboratory, and Clinical Activities for Teacher Education

Classroom, Laboratory, and Clinical Activities for Teacher Education

William E. Klingele

University of Arkansas

Allyn and Bacon, Inc.
Boston London Sydney Toronto

Series Editor: *Susanne F. Canavan*
Production Administrator: *Jane Schulman*
Editorial Services: *Susan Freese*
Text Designer: *Denise Hoffman*
Cover Coordinator: *Linda K. Dickinson*
Cover Designer: *Linda Enrico*

Library of Congress Cataloging-in-Publication Data

Klingele, William E., 1944–
   Classroom, laboratory, and clinical activities for teacher education.

   1. Teachers colleges—United States—Curricula—Hand-books, manuals, etc.   2. Student teaching—United States —Handbooks, manuals, etc.   3. Laboratory schools— United States—Curricula—Handbooks, manuals, etc. 4. Activity programs in education—United States— Handbooks, manuals, etc.   I. Title.

   LB1739.K44   1987   370'.7'33   86-10889
   ISBN 0-205-10264-6

Printed in the United States of America
10 9 8 7 6 5 4 3 2 1   90 89 88 87 86

CONTENTS

Chapter Seven
Career Awareness

PREFACE

In recent years, the need for a more realistic professional teaching experience has been demonstrated, thus making it a demand of teacher candidates and a high priority of teacher education programs. In fact, the new standards for accreditation established by the National Council for Accreditation of Teacher Education document the importance of such experience, along with the need for providing extensive and accountable teacher preparation. Far too often in the past, these learning experiences have been undefined and unaccountable. Such a misguided approach is no longer acceptable.

In an attempt to meet these changing needs, teacher education programs and accrediting agencies have evolved accordingly, emphasizing the sequential development of teaching skills, continuous integration of field experiences with formal course work, and well-coordinated, supervised, and extended field experiences beginning early in the student's education program. The overall concern is for a teacher preparation program that provides real and practical teaching experiences throughout. Thus, observation and analysis activities have become the focus of the initial phases of teacher preparation.

The Purpose of this Book

This handbook presents a practical approach to field-based laboratory activities, providing real and practical teaching experiences within a teacher education program. In Part One, *Teacher Competencies,* performance objectives are discussed, outlining three general areas of teacher preparation: foundations, instruction, and management. The student is encouraged to study these objectives carefully before beginning the actual activities presented later in the book.

In Part Two, *Observation and Analysis Activities,* laboratory experiences are provided to correspond with the competencies and objectives outlined in Part One. Along this line, the activities are divided into three sections: Chapter One, *Foundations;* Chapter Two, *Instruction;* and Chapter Three, *Management.* The activity tasks in each section are developed so that they may be used effectively within an individualized competency based program or within a traditional course context. The overall completion of these activities may be determined according to public school accessibility, the strengths and weaknesses of individual students, and the level and subject specialization of the teacher candidates. A Checksheet is provided at the end of Part Two to help students record their progress in completing the activities.

In Part Three, *Decision Activities*, students are given the opportunity to deal with the real issues and problems facing education today. Four sections of decision activities are provided: Chapter Four, *Critical Comments*; Chapter Five, *Educational Dilemmas*; Chapter Six, *Professional Decision Making*; and Chapter Seven, *Career Awareness*. These activities help students determine their individual interests and identify their potential success in the career of teaching as they participate in both individual and group exercises. Moreover, these activities complement those in Part Two by providing the chance to internalize and reinforce what is learned in the laboratory experiences.

The learning activities provided in this handbook are designed to be used on a selective basis, considering the needs of the individuals, schools, and programs involved. These activities are practical experiences that have been found to be applied easily by personnel in teacher preparation programs and public schools. The role of each individual involved—the teacher education field supervisor, the public school cooperating teacher, and the teacher candidate—is specifically outlined, indicating what is to be done and how the individual is to be held accountable.

The classroom, laboratory, and clinical activities presented in this handbook are in no way completely representative of a total teacher preparation program. This handbook merely offers an effective tool in developing and implementing such a program.

Acknowledgments

Many people have helped in the preparation of this book. In particular, I wish to thank those individuals who reviewed my work over various stages: Alan H. Eder (Northern Arizona University); Jacqueline Hultquist (Central Missouri State University); Dwane Kingery (North Texas State University); Ralph Martin (Ohio University); Morgan G. Otis (California State University—Sacramento); Clement Seldin (University of Massachusetts—Amherst); and Jack Stirton (San Joaquin Delta College).

Classroom, Laboratory, and Clinical Activities for Teacher Education

PART ONE

TEACHER COMPETENCIES

To become a competent teacher, you must be adequately prepared in the content that is to be taught. But is that enough? Is a good teacher competent in anything besides subject area? One might answer that the best teachers are those who just seem to have a natural instinct for teaching; they understand and relate to students. But what also makes a difference?

The answer is not always obvious to the observer. However, as teacher education continues to develop a research base, it becomes increasingly clear that there is a body of knowledge and skills that makes a teacher a competent professional.

As you begin a preparation program and pursue the goal of becoming a competent professional, it is helpful to examine the competencies that are part of achieving that goal. Individual teacher preparation programs identify competencies that are specific to their programs. But there are also more basic, inclusive teaching competencies that apply to teaching in general. Read the following list of basic competencies and objectives carefully before observation, analysis, and discussion activities begin.

TEACHER COMPETENCIES AND PERFORMANCE OBJECTIVES

Upon graduation, the teacher candidate will have demonstrated the knowledge, skills, attitudes, and judgment necessary to:

I. Foundations
   A. Assist students with solutions to personal, social, scholastic, educational, and occupational problems.
   1. Identify specific student problems—including personal, social, scholastic, educational, and occupational—and identify appropriate action to address each.
   2. Identify resource personnel available to aid students with personal, social, scholastic, educational, and occupational problems.
   3. Identify and describe social and psychological services available in the school system.
   4. Determine various student career alternatives and identify school system and community resources available to aid in student career development.
   B. Perform according to the ethical standards of the teaching profession.
   1. Describe teaching ethics and discriminate between ethical and unethical practices.

2. Identify and describe both professional and unprofessional teaching practices.

C. Communicate using appropriate and correct written and oral language.

   1. Written:
- **a.** Regularly write unit and subject lesson plans.
- **b.** Prepare neat, legible, and well-organized correspondence.
- **c.** Use correct spelling, punctuation, and syntax.
- **d.** Use professional-level diction, tone, and style, as appropriate to the situation.

   2. Oral:
- **a.** Use appropriate speech patterns that facilitate communication.
- **b.** Speak clearly and in well-modulated tones that facilitate teaching and learning.
- **c.** Phrase remarks in teaching and in student interaction to elicit student response, expansion, and thinking.
- **d.** Elect oral as well as written communication with parents.

D. Perform according to current standards of educational and professional development and contemporary social needs.

   1. Identify current social trends and educational developments.

   2. Identify and explain current professional practices.

E. Perform with respect and empathy for all learners as growing and developing human beings.

   1. Accept and respect each student as a worthwhile individual.

   2. Demonstrate respect for the dignity of the student, regardless of the value system of the teacher.

   3. Show courtesy to students.

F. Relate functionally with all types of personnel and systems within educational organizations.

   1. Demonstrate knowledge and skill in developing positive community relations.

   2. Exhibit the following characteristics in interpersonal relationships and personal attitudes:
- **a.** friendliness and courtesy.
- **b.** a good sense of humor.
- **c.** poise, maturity, and emotional stability.
- **d.** effective written and oral communication.
- **e.** positive assertiveness.
- **f.** positive interpersonal relationships with students,

parents, school physical plant personnel, and school professional staff.

   3. Identify at least two types of teacher organizations in a school system and describe their roles.

   4. Describe the following and explain their roles and purposes in the school system:

      a. grade-level organization.

      b. professional staff organization.

      c. specialized staff personnel.

      d. school board.

      e. physical plant personnel.

G. Demonstrate clear self-awareness of personal philosophical views regarding teaching and current educational issues.

   1. Formulate a personal philosophy of teaching based on knowledge of U.S. education, its history and objectives, and explain its meaning and significance.

   2. List various curriculum types and indicate personal preferences, supplying logical reasons for such preferences.

   3. Identify solutions to simulated educational problems dealing with classroom, cocurricular, and professional activities.

   4. Identify and explain current educational issues and write personal opinions regarding each.

   5. Identify local, state, and national professional organizations and their policies and functions.

   6. Identify and explain elements of school law concerning the teacher, student, and educational agency.

H. Acknowledge and apply current educational theory concerning how people learn and grow.

   1. Identify and explain methods of behavior modification and how they are used.

   2. Provide positive reinforcement for student academic achievement.

   3. Determine in-school learning experiences suitable to a given group or individual.

   4. Reinforce independent thinking.

   5. Identify Bloom's taxonomy of learning objectives.

   6. Identify the enabling performances that will permit the learner to meet final objectives.

   7. Describe learning activities that should effectively result in achievement of enabling performances and final objectives.

   8. Identify and describe students' growth and development problems.

II. Instruction

Planning:

A. Determine students' needs and goals for successful completion of a course of study.

  1. Supplement lesson plans with materials and instruction designed to meet each student's interests, needs, and abilities. Evaluation criteria include:

   a. planning differentiated assignments or expectations for individual differences.

   b. selecting and using alternative types of individualized instruction when group instruction is not functional.

  2. Through participation in small groups, identify and explain motivation techniques currently used to promote:

   a. student interest in the topic under discussion.

   b. positive student social relationships.

   c. student curiosity.

  3. Relate subject matter to the needs of students.

   a. Identify and describe the different needs of students.

   b. Explain how these different needs will be met with the instruction of a particular course of study.

B. Identify the knowledge and skills necessary to perform successfully within a given discipline, occupation, field of study, or task framework.

  1. Identify specific concepts in subject matter.

  2. Write behavioral objectives appropriate for teaching and learning these concepts.

  3. Demonstrate basic knowledge of subject vocabulary.

  4. Show the best use of available physical facilities as adaptable to elected methods of instruction.

C. Formulate and write suitable general and specific performance objectives for a given instructional plan.

D. Select and develop instructional content and an instructional plan for a specific curriculum, course, unit, and lesson, based on the following criteria:

  1. Determine course goals and objectives.

  2. Identify the unit topics for a course and lesson topics for a unit.

  3. Write a content outline for a unit.

  4. Write lesson plans to organize proposed teacher and learner activities.

  5. Estimate an approximate time frame for each unit.

E. Determine and select appropriate instructional materials, supplies, equipment, media, and aids for learning activities.

  1. Exhibit the skills and abilities to design, produce, use, and/or operate functional, good-quality media. Included

in this objective is the knowledge of how to produce and
use:
  a. overhead transparencies.
  b. posters.
  c. signs.
  d. bulletin boards.
  e. laminations.
  f. audiorecordings.
  g. 35mm slides.
  h. filmstrips.
  i. 8mm and/or 16mm films.
  j. learning activities packages (LAP).
  k. learning centers.
  l. models.
  m. simulations and games.
  n. microcomputers.
2. Demonstrate the following skills in teaching a lesson to
  students:
  a. Distribute materials and supplies.
  b. Use and care for audiovisual equipment.
F. Select appropriate teaching strategies and delivery systems.
  1. Demonstrate knowledge of various teaching procedures,
    including lecture, demonstration, questioning, debate,
    problem solving, inquiry, individual contracts, and field
    trips.
  2. Effectively implement each of the various teaching pro-
    cedures in simulated classroom situations.
  3. Modify procedures during lessons when observable feed-
    back indicates change is needed.
  4. Evaluate the appropriateness of a given teaching strategy
    to the desired outcome.

Delivering:
G. Teach lessons utilizing a variety of techniques and methods.
  1. Group classes according to needs presented.
  2. Describe the skills necessary to provide large-group,
    small-group, and individualized instruction.
  3. Identify and describe the affective, cognitive, and psycho-
    motor domains of learning.
  4. Identify questioning processes.
  5. Identify and describe verbal and nonverbal behavior.
  6. Demonstrate various presentation techniques.
  7. Identify and utilize methods of motivation.
H. Present lessons utilizing appropriate instructional materials.

1. Select, operate, and coordinate various methods, techniques, instructional material, and equipment that will help students achieve the objectives for a given instruction unit.
2. Determine if instructional devices were successful through the results of various evaluation methods.
3. Select and use instructional media, including the following:
   a. 16mm sound projector.
   b. carousel slide projector.
   c. overhead projector.
   d. opaque projector.
   e. filmstrip projector.
   f. audiotape recorder.
   g. microcomputer.

I. Supervise student classroom and laboratory experiences.
1. Classroom:
   a. Identify and maintain a physical environment suitable to various modes of special learning activities.
   b. Identify students by name.
   c. Establish a nonthreatening climate for learning and interaction.
   d. Demonstrate techniques of individualized instruction.
   e. Practice attitudes of understanding student needs and behavior.
2. Laboratory:
   a. Identify each item of equipment and describe its function and care.
   b. Identify safety practices.
   c. Demonstrate individual lab procedures, as indicated in daily lesson plans.
   d. List weekly tallies of supplies, items, and equipment.

Evaluating:
J. Design an evaluation plan based on an analysis of representative program material.
1. After having presented and taught the program material, construct appropriate tests for evaluation, including the following test types:
   a. true/false.
   b. completion.
   c. matching.
   d. skills.
   e. essay.

      f. short-answer.

      g. multiple-choice.

  2. Observe students' verbal behavior in relation to the program material.

  3. Provide a choice of appropriate projects that will demonstrate the students' understanding and knowledge of the program material.

K. Evaluate student progress and provide constructive feedback.

  1. Provide immediate test results and interpretations.

  2. Identify and implement various methods of statistical test analysis.

  3. Demonstrate knowledge of time constraints.

L. Establish and carry out a self-evaluation of teaching.

  1. Utilize Flander's Interaction Analysis or a similar method of self-evaluation.

  2. Demonstrate the ability to use videotape equipment for a self-evaluating process.

III. Management

A. Identify and implement systems that produce desired changes in student behavior.

  1. Explain desirable classroom behavior to students.

  2. Identify problem behavior.

  3. Demonstrate the ability to work with all students as individuals.

  4. Identify possible contributing factors that influence students' personalities.

  5. Develop positive reinforcement for appropriate behavior.

B. Design and define operating responsibilities for both the learner and the teacher.

  1. Identify and explain classroom procedures and regulations to students.

  2. Design students' learning activities so that each student demonstrates positive growth in functional behavior.

  3. Design appropriate tasks to be completed by students to attain a given objective.

  4. Organize and encourage students to operate the classroom in an orderly and efficient manner.

  5. Exercise positive discipline so that all students profit from the learning environment.

  6. Provide students with written explanation of the above proceedings.

C. Provide acceptable physical management of the learning environment.
  1. Organize and distribute necessary supplies for students' learning activities.
  2. Determine desirable physical characteristics conducive to an effective learning environment.
D. Establish and utilize regular procedures for the acquisition, safe use, storage, and maintenance of equipment, supplies, and other materials.
  1. Describe the procedure for obtaining instructional materials.
  2. Develop accessible, appropriate, flexible, and safe units of storage for resource and reference materials.
  3. Operate all media equipment correctly and safely.
E. Appropriately supervise noninstructional activities.
  1. Identify the administrative policies concerning noninstructional activities.
  2. Describe student roles concerning noninstructional activities.
  3. List and incorporate student ideas into noninstructional activities.
F. Prepare appropriate records and reports.
  1. Identify what forms are needed for recording and reporting.
  2. Complete all records and reports accurately and submit them to the proper individual at the required time.

PART TWO

OBSERVATION
AND ANALYSIS
ACTIVITIES

As a student enrolled in the laboratory phases of teacher preparation, you will benefit substantially by observing and participating in public school classrooms. This opportunity provides you with a superior method of testing yourself as a potential teacher and also provides specific exercises to aid in your development of teaching competencies. Moreover, coordinating program instruction with actual field experience will enhance your preparation as a teacher.

While performing the learning tasks described in the following pages, you will play various roles, including those of observer, participant, and analyst. In addition to what you will learn by observing and analyzing public school education, you will also provide a useful service to the school or program in which you are participating.

The learning activities described in Part Two are separated into three basic areas of teacher preparation: *foundations, instruction,* and *management.* For each learning activity, you will be given a specified *performance objective,* along with a number of *performance tasks.* How well you complete a given number of performance tasks will determine your success in completing the performance objective for each activity.

Each of the three basic areas of learning activities is preceded by a list of teaching competencies, which represent the general goals of teacher education programs. The learning tasks in each area are designed to help you work toward these specified competencies. You may find it helpful to refer to these competencies from time to time while you are participating in laboratory activities.

DIRECTIONS FOR COMPLETING LEARNING ACTIVITIES

Fifty-four learning activities are presented in three sections: foundations (**F**), instruction (**I**), and management (**M**). For anyone to complete all of the learning activities would certainly be a comprehensive endeavor. But more importantly, such a comprehensive approach would ignore individual needs and situations. Learning activities should be selected on the basis of your own needs, the design of the teacher education program, the grade level or subject-area major, and the circumstances surrounding the school site. An individualized program of learning activities should be prescribed for each teacher candidate (TC).

The performance tasks that correspond to each performance objective are listed in order of difficulty, from simple to more complex. The number and type of performance tasks you complete should also be determined on an individual basis, considering the factors outlined above. Again, each TC should be prescribed his or her own course.

The activities prescribed are appropriate at elementary, middle, and secondary levels. When the letter (**P**) is included following the learning activity name, some prerequisite research or instruction may be needed for completion.

Your responses to the performance tasks should be brief and concise and written on the learning activity sheets when possible. If additional pages are needed, attach them to the learning activity sheet and submit the materials together.

CHAPTER ONE

FOUNDATIONS

Foundations Competencies

Upon certification, the teacher candidate will have demonstrated the knowledge, skills, attitudes, and judgment necessary to:

1. Assist students with solutions to personal, social, scholastic, educational, and occupational problems.
2. Perform according to the ethical procedures of the teaching profession.
3. Communicate using appropriate and correct written and oral language.
4. Perform according to current standards of educational and professional development and contemporary social needs.
5. Perform with respect and empathy for all learners as growing and developing human beings.
6. Relate functionally with all types of personnel and systems within educational organizations.
7. Demonstrate a clear self-awareness of personal philosophical views regarding teaching and current educational issues.
8. Acknowledge and apply current educational theory concerning how people learn and grow.

Students' Personal Problems

Performance Objective

After completing classroom observation, the TC should be able to identify a student with a personal problem, determine what the problem is, and assist in reaching a solution.

Performance Tasks

1. Carefully observe the teaching-learning encounter in a given classroom. When you feel you are ready, identify a student who seems to have a specific personal problem. If possible, check with the classroom teacher to see if he or she concurs. Briefly describe the problem.

2. After you have identified and described the student's problem, seek resources (individuals and materials) to find solutions. List your resources and briefly describe your solutions.

DATE COMPLETED_____   SUPERVISOR'S SIGNATURE_____

Notes

Students' Social Problems

Performance Objective

After completing classroom observation, the TC should be able to identify a student who has a social problem, determine what the problem is, and assist in reaching a solution.

Performance Tasks

1. Carefully observe the teaching-learning encounter in a given classroom. When you feel you are ready, identify a student who seems to have a specific social problem. If possible, check with the teacher to see if he or she concurs. Briefly describe the problem.

2. After you have identified and described the student's problem, seek resources (individuals and materials) to find solutions. List your resources and briefly describe your solutions.

Notes

Students'
Scholastic Problems

Performance Objective

After completing classroom observation, the TC should be able to identify a student who has a learning problem, determine what the problem is, and assist in reaching a solution.

Performance Tasks

1. Carefully observe the teaching-learning encounter in a given classroom. When you feel you are ready, identify a student who seems to have a specific learning problem. If possible, check with the teacher to see if he or she concurs. Briefly describe the problem.

2. After you have identified and described the student's problem, seek out resources (individuals and materials) to find solutions. List your resources and briefly identify your solutions.

Notes

Students' Occupational Problems (P)

Performance Objective

After completing classroom observation, the TC should be able to select a student who needs occupational guidance and provide occupational information and direction.

Performance Tasks

1. After carefully observing the teaching-learning encounter in a given classroom, select a student who you feel may benefit from receiving occupational advice. Describe how the student displays the need for such assistance.

2. Develop a personalized plan or process for assisting the student with career choices. Outline this plan briefly.

3. After three weeks, talk with the student again about his or her occupational interests. Help construct a personal plan listing what qualities and preparation are needed for a specific career; also describe the career, listing advantages and disadvantages for the future.

DATE COMPLETED_____ SUPERVISOR'S SIGNATURE_____

Notes

Teacher Ethics

Performance Objective

After a three-week period of school observation, the TC should be able to describe teacher ethics and identify practices that are unethical.

Performance Tasks

1. After a three-week period of observation, reflect on the types of teacher performance you have seen. Without specifically identifying anyone, prepare a list of practices that you feel are unethical as they occurred or appeared to have occurred in the classroom, in the teachers' lounge, at other places in the school, or in the community.

2. Write a sentence describing how you feel about each of the following teacher practices:
   a. discussing problem students in the teachers' lounge.
   b. smoking in front of students.
   c. expressing personal positions on controversial social, political, and religious issues to students.

3. In one paragraph, state a personal code of ethics for teachers.

DATE COMPLETED_____   SUPERVISOR'S SIGNATURE_____

Notes

Teacher Professionalism

Performance Objective

After a three-week period of school observation, the TC should be able to identify characteristics of teacher professionalism and distinguish between professional and nonprofessional character and performance.

Performance Tasks

1. Observe the in-class and out-of-class activities, personalities, and general behavior of several teachers for a minimum of three weeks. Choose the two teachers with whom you have become the most familiar. Compare the two, briefly describing their similarities and differences. (Do not name the teachers.)

2. Rank the two teachers based on your perception of their professionalism. Prepare contrasting lists describing professional and nonprofessional attitudes and practices of teachers in general.

3. Write a one-page essay on "The Truly Professional Teacher."

DATE COMPLETED_____   SUPERVISOR'S SIGNATURE_____

Notes

Teacher Language Communications

Performance Objective

After performing as a teacher assistant, the TC should be able to identify his or her language communication strengths and weaknesses.

Performance Tasks

1. On a one-to-one basis, help a student learn something that he or she finds difficult. Tape-record the session and later evaluate the communications involved, including voice quality and language usage.

2. Play the tape recording to three of your colleagues. Ask them to critique you. Describe their responses.

3. Videotape your performance in a one-to-one or group teaching experience. Later, play back the tape and evaluate your language communication, listing both strengths and weaknesses.

Strengths	Weaknesses
1.	1.
2.	2.
3.	3.
4.	4.

DATE COMPLETED_____   SUPERVISOR'S SIGNATURE_____

Notes

Schedules

Performance Objective

Given the opportunity to observe and participate in a public school, the TC should be able to describe and analyze a typical master schedule, teacher schedule, and student schedule.

Performance Tasks

1. Look at the school's master schedule. Discuss how and why the schedule was constructed with the person who prepared it. Then list the major considerations involved in planning a master schedule.

2. Observe the daily or weekly schedule of a given teacher. List those factors the teacher apparently considered in scheduling instruction and other activities. Check with the teacher to see if he or she actually considered these factors. Place a checkmark next to the factors that the teacher did consider.

3. Consider how you would function according to another teacher's schedule and write a paragraph describing how you would operate. How would you change the schedule to make it more appropriate or convenient for your life goals and instructional style?

DATE COMPLETED_____   SUPERVISOR'S SIGNATURE_____

Notes

Curriculum (P)

Performance Objective

Given the opportunity to observe and participate in a public school, the TC should be able to define and describe the relationships between curriculum, course of study, curriculum guides, and instructional plans.

Performance Tasks

1. Define *curriculum*. List components of the curriculum in the school in which you are observing.

2. Describe the course of study within the school in which you are involved.

3. Review a curriculum guide and outline what it contains.

4. List topics for instructional units that would relate to a given course in a curriculum guide.

5. In a paragraph, describe the relationship among a course of study, curriculum guide, instructional plans, and a daily schedule.

Notes

Attitude Observations

Performance Objective

After completing classroom observation, the TC should be able to identify the general attitudes of the teacher and the students and provide suggestions for improving both.

Performance Tasks

1. Carefully observe the teaching-learning atmosphere in a classroom. Briefly describe the teacher's general attitude toward students and his or her job in general. Does the teacher appear to be generally happy with his or her work or simply tolerating it?

2. Put yourself in the teacher's position and think of the future. Describe yourself in that position 10 years from now. Do you think you will be happy or simply tolerating what you are doing? Explain.

3. Based on your observations of the classroom, describe what changes could be made to facilitate a happier and healthier atmosphere for both teachers and students.

4. What specific responsibilities, if any, do you think a public school system has regarding student mental health?

DATE COMPLETED_____   SUPERVISOR'S SIGNATURE_____

Notes

School System Organization (P)

Performance Objective

Given the opportunity for public school observation, the TC should be able to describe and explain the administrative, grade-level, and physical plant organization of the given school system.

Performance Tasks

1. Prepare a chart of the persons and positions in the school system, showing their organizational relationships. Include the school board at the top of the chart and the students at the bottom.

2. In one sentence, describe the role of each position at the various levels of the school system.

DATE COMPLETED_____   SUPERVISOR'S SIGNATURE_____

Notes

Student Guidance

Performance Objective

Given the opportunity to observe and question a practicing guidance counselor, the TC should be able to identify and describe the basic services of the guidance staff and their relationship to other school personnel.

Performance Tasks

1. List the basic services of the guidance program in the school.

2. Identify which services the guidance staff perform most often in the school in which you are observing.

3. Describe the classroom teacher's responsibility for guidance. How much responsibility should he or she have?

DATE COMPLETED_____ SUPERVISOR'S SIGNATURE_____

Notes

The School Board (P)

Performance Objective

Given the opportunity to observe a school board meeting, the TC should be able to describe the role, responsibility, and practices of a school board.

Performance Tasks

1. Attend a school board meeting. List the officers and members of the board and indicate how each attained this position.

2. Briefly describe the meeting's agenda and any significant transactions that were made.

3. Prepare a list of the school board's duties and legal responsibilities.

DATE COMPLETED_____   SUPERVISOR'S SIGNATURE_____

Notes

Teacher Organizations (P)

Performance Objective

Given the opportunity to observe public school organization, the TC should be able to identify the names, types, roles, responsibilities, and practices of teacher organizations operant in a given school system.

Performance Tasks

1. Prepare a list of the teacher organizations you have found in the school system in which you are observing and categorize them according to purpose.

2. List other teacher organizations in other school systems with which you are familiar. Identify the purpose of each.

3. Attend a meeting of a professional teacher organization and describe the agenda and transactions. What were your personal feelings about the meeting?

DATE COMPLETED_____ SUPERVISOR'S SIGNATURE_____

Notes

Parent Perception

Performance Objective

Given the opportunity to observe and assist in a public school classroom, the TC should be able to describe a particular student as the parent perceives him or her and as the teacher perceives him or her.

Performance Tasks

1. Reflect back on your own schooling and select one of your former teachers. Indicate how you think that teacher would have described you at that time. How would one or both of your parents have described you at the same time?

2. How much parent-teacher communication is desirable? Support your answer.

3. Observe a parent-teacher conference. Is the parent's perception of the child consistent with the teacher's apparent perception? What is your perception of the child?

DATE COMPLETED_____ SUPERVISOR'S SIGNATURE_____

Notes

Issue: Teaching as a Profession (P)

Performance Objective

Given a list of professional criteria and provided with the opportunity for public school observation, the TC should be able to evaluate whether or not teaching is a profession, citing specific examples to support his or her thesis.

Performance Tasks

1. Using a foundations textbook, prepare a list of the criteria that determine professionalism. Based on this list, analyze teaching, indicating which criteria teaching satisfies. Explain your reasoning.

2. Based on your observation of various public school personnel, cite specific examples that you feel qualify or disqualify teaching as a profession. Cite an example for each of the criteria you listed above.

3. Indicate what changes in public school operation would make teaching more professional.

DATE COMPLETED_____   SUPERVISOR'S SIGNATURE_____

Notes

Issue: Accountability (P)

Performance Objective

Given the opportunity for public school observation, the TC should be able to define and illustrate *accountability*, as perceived in a given public school system.

Performance Tasks

1. Define *accountability* and list at least three ways that it has been implemented by public school systems, state departments, and teacher organizations.

2. Describe the approach to accountability taken by the school system in which you are participating.

3. Explain how the teachers you have observed are being held accountable.

4. Indicate how public school systems and individual classroom teachers should be held accountable. Explain.

DATE COMPLETED_____   SUPERVISOR'S SIGNATURE_____

Notes

Students' Physical Development

Performance Objective

After completing classroom observation, the TC should be able to describe the physical extent of student growth and cite specific learning implications for the levels of growth identified.

Performance Tasks

1. Observe a class for a minimum of 40 minutes. Group students into the following categories: Boys—tall, Boys—short, Girls—tall, Girls—short, Boys—overweight, Boys—underweight, Girls—overweight, Girls—underweight, Boys—average weight and height, Girls—average weight and height.

2. Analyze the results of your categorization by counting the number of students in each category. Describe the physically typical girl and boy in the class.

3. Describe the girl and the boy in the class possessing the most extreme physical variations. Describe their social relationship to their teacher and their peers.

4. Describe any specific learning difficulties displayed by the two students possessing extreme physical variations.

Continued

DATE COMPLETED_____ SUPERVISOR'S SIGNATURE_____

5. List apparent teaching and learning implications pertaining to the physical development of students.

Notes

Multicultural Activity 1

Performance Objective

After completing public school observation, the TC should be able to identify culturally different components of a school and instructional situation.

Performance Tasks

1. Observe a public school facility. List the facilities, activities, events, and the like that pertain to different student backgrounds within the school.

2. Observe a minimum of three instructional situations. Identify the methods, materials, and curriculum that relate to different student backgrounds.

3. Identify additional school or class activities that could help a culturally different student population be recognized.

DATE COMPLETED_____   SUPERVISOR'S SIGNATURE_____

Notes

Multicultural Activity 2 (P)

Performance Objective

After completing public school observation, the TC should be able to identify those cultural differences that are apparent among students in the classroom.

Performance Tasks

1. List at least one myth or stereotype associated with each of three different cultural/ethnic groups.

2. Select and observe a particular cultural/ethnic group of students. Describe how these students are unique as to linguistic variations, learning styles, and cultural variations. How are these differences felt in the classroom?

Notes

Special Students 1

Performance Objective

After completing public school observation, the TC should be able to identify the facilities, activities, and special programs available for the special student.

Performance Tasks

1. Observe a public school facility. Identify the facilities, activities, events, and special programs designed for gifted and physically or mentally handicapped students.

2. Observe a minimum of five specific learning situations. Identify the special provisions for gifted and physically or mentally handicapped students that were used by the teacher(s).

3. Identify alternative or additional facilities, activities, and programs that could be provided for special students.

DATE COMPLETED_____   SUPERVISOR'S SIGNATURE_____

Notes

Special Students 2

Performance Objective

After completing public school observation, the TC should be able to identify both personal and observable peer feelings about handicapped students and suggest methods for overcoming any negative views.

Performance Tasks

1. Observe a minimum of four classes that contain mainstream physically or mentally handicapped students. What would be your initial feeling about having these students in your class?

2. In general, identify how the teachers you observed treated the handicapped students. How did the other students treat them?

3. Identify what you could do as a teacher to best prepare yourself, the general student population, the mainstreamed student population, and the instructional climate for mainstreaming.

DATE COMPLETED_____   SUPERVISOR'S SIGNATURE_____

Notes

CHAPTER TWO
INSTRUCTION

Instruction Competencies

Upon certification, the teacher candidate will have demonstrated the knowledge, skills, attitudes, and judgment necessary to:

Planning:
1. Determine students' needs and goals for successful completion of a course of study.
2. Identify the knowledge and skills necessary to perform successfully within a given discipline, occupation, field of study, or task framework.
3. Formulate educational objectives.
4. Select and develop instructional content and an instructional plan for a specific curriculum, course, unit, and lesson.
5. Determine and select appropriate instructional materials, supplies, equipment, media, and aids for learning activities.
6. Select appropriate teaching strategies and delivery systems.

Delivering:
7. Teach lessons utilizing a variety of techniques and methods.
8. Present lessons utilizing appropriate instructional materials.
9. Supervise student classroom, clinical, and laboratory experiences.

Evaluating:
10. Design evaluation plans based on an analysis of representative program material.
11. Evaluate student progress and provide constructive feedback.
12. Establish and carry out a self-evaluation of teaching.

The Instructional Process

Performance Objective

After completing classroom observation, the TC should be able to analyze the instructional process: what the teacher was trying to teach, how the teacher was teaching, how students were learning, and how it could be discerned that learning was taking place.

Performance Tasks

1. Observe a lesson being taught. Identify the instructional content.

2. List activities that students were required to do to learn the content.

3. List the activities or events performed by the teacher to facilitate student learning.

4. Identify the means used by the teacher to determine if the students were learning the content.

DATE COMPLETED_____   SUPERVISOR'S SIGNATURE_____

Notes

Instructional Strategies

Performance Objective

After completing classroom observation, the TC should be able to identify and describe specific classroom techniques and methods suitable to a given level and teaching content area.

Performance Tasks

1. Observe a minimum of four teacher lessons in the same class. Prepare a list of instructional units, describing the content area taught and grade levels involved.

2. Outline how the teacher proceeded in teaching each unit observed.

3. Specify the processes that appeared to be the most successful. Briefly explain your choices.

4. Specify the processes that appeared to be unsuccessful. Again, briefly explain your choices.

5. Prepare an outline of an alternative process to one of the processes that you observed.

DATE COMPLETED_____   SUPERVISOR'S SIGNATURE_____

Notes

Motivation 1

Performance Objective

After completing classroom observation, the TC should be able
to identify levels of student motivation and suggest ways of
improving it.

Performance Tasks

1. Observe a lesson being taught. How interested do students
seem to be in what they are being taught?

_____ very interested   _____ interested

_____ somewhat interested   _____ not interested

2. How pleasant are most students in the learning situation?

_____ very pleasant   _____ pleasant

_____ somewhat pleasant   _____ unpleasant

3. How much success do students seem to be having in learning
the content?

_____ much success   _____ little success

_____ moderate success   _____ no success

Continued

DATE COMPLETED_____   SUPERVISOR'S SIGNATURE_____

4. Indicate the number of students in the class that appear to be motivated to the following degrees:

_____ extremely motivated   _____ slightly motivated

_____ moderately motivated   _____ not motivated

Notes

Motivation 2

Performance Objective

After completing classroom observation, the TC should be able to identify motivation techniques and suggest appropriate motivational devices.

Performance Tasks

1. Observe a teaching-learning activity. List techniques used by the teacher to motivate students.

2. Identify other motivational techniques that would be appropriate for this particular lesson.

3. Identify a student in the classroom who doesn't seem to be responding to the teacher's motivational techniques. Propose an individualized motivational technique that may be desirable for the identified student and explain how it should be implemented.

DATE COMPLETED_____   SUPERVISOR'S SIGNATURE_____

Notes

Student Interests

Performance Objective

After completing classroom observation, the TC should be able to identify the relationship between content and student interests and suggest ways of relating the two.

Performance Tasks

1. Observe a teaching-learning situation. Identify ways in which the teacher has related the subject to the students' interests.

2. Identify other possible ways in which the given subject area could be related to the real world of the students.

3. Propose highly novel or creative ways in which the subject area observed could be presented to better relate it to student interests.

Notes

Reinforcement (P)

Performance Objective

After observing a teaching-learning situation, the TC should be able to identify verbal and nonverbal reinforcement and suggest suitable means of providing both.

Performance Tasks

1. Observe a teaching-learning situation. Prepare two lists, one recording observed verbal reinforcement comments made by the teacher and one recording nonverbal reinforcement actions made by the teacher.

2. List those verbal and nonverbal actions that appeared to be most effective.

3. Identify other verbal and nonverbal reinforcement actions that you feel would be effective.

DATE COMPLETED_____   SUPERVISOR'S SIGNATURE_____

Notes

Transfer of Learning (P)

Performance Objective

After observing a teaching-learning situation, the TC should be able to recognize techniques for facilitating transfer and suggest alternative methods of doing so.

Performance Tasks

1. *Transfer* occurs when past learning influences new learning. Observe a teaching-learning situation and identify what the teacher does to facilitate transfer. List anything that you think may have facilitated transfer.

2. Identify how each of the following techniques facilitates transfer:
   a. pointing out the similarity of the new content to already learned content.
   b. associating the new content with content that is generally associated with old content.
   c. specifying the dissimilarities between new and old content that may be emphasized.

3. Identify additional ways of facilitating transfer.

Notes

Discussion

Performance Objective

Given the opportunity for public school classroom observation, the TC should be able to identify those practices and techniques that produce successful class discussions.

Performance Tasks

1. Observe a teaching-learning activity that emphasizes student discussion. Specify the topic of the discussion.

2. Record the questions the teacher used to stimulate the discussion. Indicate which questions were successful or unsuccessful in producing student discussion.

3. Describe the specific techniques (other than the questions asked) the teacher used to stimulate discussion.

4. Describe the purposes of classroom discussion.

DATE COMPLETED_____   SUPERVISOR'S SIGNATURE_____

Notes

Nonverbal Behavior

Performance Objective

Given the opportunity for public school classroom observation, the TC should be able to identify how teachers' nonverbal behavior facilitates or obstructs learning.

Performance Tasks

1. Observe a teaching-learning activity in which there is a considerable amount of teacher participation. Prepare a list of the teacher's nonverbal behaviors, including gestures, facial expressions, nods, smiles, and the like. Indicate the approximate number of times each behavior is displayed (30-minute activity).

2. Observe a teaching-learning activity for an additional 30 minutes. Observe the teacher's nonverbal behaviors, as well as the students' response to them. Record your observations.

3. Indicate which nonverbal behaviors tend to facilitate learning and which do not. Support your answers.

DATE COMPLETED_____   SUPERVISOR'S SIGNATURE_____

Notes

Verbal Behavior

Performance Objective

Given the opportunity for public school classroom observation, the TC should be able to identify how teachers' verbal behavior facilitates or obstructs learning.

Performance Tasks

1. Observe a 10-minute teaching-learning activity in which the teacher does a considerable amount of talking. Prepare a list of the types of "teacher talk," using the following categories: (a) giving directions; (b) lecturing—providing information; (c) questioning; (d) praising or encouraging; and (e) other. Record the approximate number of teacher statements that belong in each category.

2. Choose one teacher statement or question from each category. Indicate the student response to each.

3. Indicate which types of teacher verbal behavior tend to facilitate learning and which do not.

DATE COMPLETED_____   SUPERVISOR'S SIGNATURE_____

Notes

Questioning

Performance Objective

After completing classroom observation, the TC should be able to identify various types of teacher questions and categorize them accordingly.

Performance Tasks

1. Observe a teaching-learning activity in which the teacher does a considerable amount of questioning. Identify the number of "teacher questions" observed in each of the following categories:

    a. fact questions (calling for details, specifics, etc.)   ____

    b. concepts (building relationships between ideas and pulling together generalizations)   ____

    c. values (linking facts and concepts to the choices and decisions in the students' lives)   ____

2. Categorize the teacher's questions into the following two areas, indicating the number of each:

threatening ____   nonthreatening ____

3. In a paragraph, describe how teacher questions influence learning.

DATE COMPLETED_____ SUPERVISOR'S SIGNATURE_____

Notes

Large-group Instruction

Performance Objective

Given the opportunity for public school classroom observation
and participation, the TC should be able to prepare and carry
out a large-group instructional activity for a given group of
students.

Performance Tasks

1. Assist in planning and delivering a large-group instructional
activity. Describe the plan and the teaching-learning experiences. Indicate the apparent effectiveness of the experiences.

2. Outline an instructional plan for a large group of students.
Include specific objectives, as well as media, activities, and
evaluation. Obtain the cooperating teacher's approval of the
plan.

3. After receiving approval from the cooperating teacher, teach
one lesson as planned.

4. In a paragraph, indicate the apparent success or failure of the
instruction, giving specific reasons for your feelings.

DATE COMPLETED_____ SUPERVISOR'S SIGNATURE_____

Notes

Small-group Instruction

Performance Objective

Given the opportunity for public school classroom observation and participation, the TC should be able to prepare and carry out a small-group instructional activity for a given group of students.

Performance Tasks

1. Assist in planning and delivering a small-group instructional activity. Describe the plan and the teaching-learning experiences. Indicate the apparent effectiveness of the experiences.

2. Prepare an instructional plan for a small group of students. Include specific objectives, as well as media, activities, and evaluation. Obtain the cooperating teacher's approval of the plan.

3. After receiving approval from the cooperating teacher, teach the lesson as planned.

4. In a paragraph, indicate the apparent success or failure of the instruction, giving specific reasons for your feelings.

DATE COMPLETED_____   SUPERVISOR'S SIGNATURE_____

Notes

Tutoring

Performance Objective

Given the opportunity for public school classroom observation and participation, the TC should be able to identify a student who has a learning problem and then prepare and carry out an appropriate individualized teacher-learner instructional activity.

Performance Tasks

1. Observe a teaching-learning activity. Identify a student who appears to have difficulty learning the instructional content being taught in the given activity situation. Confirm your selection with the teacher.

2. Obtain permission from the teacher to work individually with the identified student. Prepare an instructional plan for assisting the student with the instructional content that he or she is having difficulty with.

3. After receiving the teacher's approval, implement the plan.

4. In a paragraph, indicate the apparent success or failure of the individualized instruction. Give specific reasons for your feelings.

DATE COMPLETED_____   SUPERVISOR'S SIGNATURE_____

Notes

Educational Media

Performance Objective

Given the opportunity for public school classroom observation and participation, the TC should be able to identify various procedures and applications of educational media and assist in their production and use.

Performance Tasks

1. Observe a minimum of three hours of teaching-learning experiences. Prepare a list of all the media utilized in the activities. Include such things as bulletin boards, exhibits, models, projectors, filmstrips, slides, motion pictures, recorders, phonographs, TV, programmed instruction, and chalkboards.

2. Describe how each type of media was used and how it apparently affected learning.

3. Assist teachers in utilizing as many types of media as possible. Prepare a list of these media, describing how each was used.

DATE COMPLETED_____   SUPERVISOR'S SIGNATURE_____

Notes

Planning (P)

Performance Objective

Given the opportunity for public school classroom observation, the TC should be able to identify a given instructional plan, as well as prepare his or her own instructional plan for a given learning experience.

Performance Tasks

1. Observe a teaching-learning experience. Prepare a report outlining the apparent instructional plan being followed by the teacher. Check with the teacher and compare his or her plan with what you have observed.

2. Assist the teacher in preparing an instructional plan for another teaching-learning activity. Obtain a copy of the plan and analyze it carefully. Then observe the teacher and describe how he or she carried out the plan.

3. Obtain from the teacher a list of the instructional content to be taught within a 30-minute to 2-hour time span. Prepare an appropriate instructional plan for the content identified and time allotted.

DATE COMPLETED_____ SUPERVISOR'S SIGNATURE_____

Notes

Determining Group Experiences

Performance Objective

After a two-week period of public school classroom observation, the TC should be able to identify group experiences aimed at student learning of the given content.

Performance Tasks

1. Observe a teaching-learning situation. List what appear to be the objectives of the lesson.

2. Identify and describe the large- or small-group experiences the teacher is using to teach the identified content.

3. Identify which experiences appear to be most effective; specify your reasons. Also identify which experiences appear to be least effective; specify your reasons.

4. Identify and describe one large-group activity and one small-group activity that may be effective in teaching the identified content and have not been used by the teacher observed.

DATE COMPLETED_____   SUPERVISOR'S SIGNATURE_____

Notes

Determining Individual Experiences

Performance Objective

After a two-week period of public school classroom observation, the TC should be able to identify individual experiences aimed at student learning of the given content.

Performance Tasks

1. Observe a teacher providing individualized instruction. Identify the objectives and/or content the teacher is covering during your observation.

2. Identify and describe the individualized experiences the teacher is using to teach the identified content.

3. Identify which experiences appear to be most effective; specify your reasons. Also identify which experiences appear to be least effective; specify your reasons.

4. Identify and describe two types of individualized activities that may be effective in teaching the identified content and have not been utilized by the teacher observed.

DATE COMPLETED_____   SUPERVISOR'S SIGNATURE_____

Notes

Determining Career Competencies

Performance Objective

Given the opportunity for public school classroom observation and data collection, the TC should be able to prepare a list of competencies for a selected career, assess how instructional content relates to a selected career, and demonstrate this relation to students.

Performance Tasks

1. Observe a minimum of six learning sessions. Prepare a list of the content that was covered in some way.

2. Prepare a list of the careers to which the content in the observed sessions might be applied.

3. Identify how a teacher might relate the content covered in the observed classes to specific careers. How can this relation be demonstrated to students?

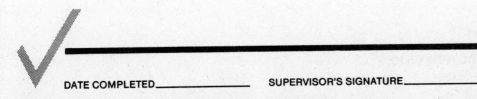

DATE COMPLETED_____ SUPERVISOR'S SIGNATURE_____

Notes

Instructional Objectives (P)

Performance Objective

Given the opportunity for public school classroom observation and individual or group instruction concerning instructional objectives, the TC should be able to prepare instructional objectives for a given instructional plan.

Performance Tasks

1. Observe a teaching-learning activity and prepare a list of what appear to be the objectives of the activity.

2. Take your preliminary list of objectives and write them in specific terms. In particular, indicate what the students should be able to do after receiving instruction.

3. Describe what types of evaluative activities might be used to assess whether the students have accomplished these performance objectives.

4. Obtain from the teacher an instructional plan for a given teaching-learning experience. Prepare a list of performance objectives for the plan.

DATE COMPLETED_____ SUPERVISOR'S SIGNATURE_____

Notes

Evaluation

Performance Objective

Given the opportunity for public school classroom observation, the TC should be able to evaluate a teacher-made evaluation instrument and a commercial test according to a given set of criteria.

Performance Tasks

1. Observe a classroom during a testing situation in which a teacher-made test is used. Describe what the teacher said and did during the evaluation.

2. Obtain a copy of the teacher-made test. Determine what the test is supposed to measure. Consult the instructional objectives, if possible. Do the test items measure what they are supposed to measure?

3. Obtain a copy of a commercially prepared test. Determine what the test is supposed to measure. Read the test items. Do they measure what they are supposed to measure? List any questions that a member of a culturally different group may have difficulty with because of language, values, experiences, and the like.

4. Using what you have learned through reviewing other tests, develop a test of your own.

DATE COMPLETED_____   SUPERVISOR'S SIGNATURE_____

Notes

Multicultural Instruction

Performance Objective

After three weeks of public school classroom observation, the TC should be able to identify and plan instructional techniques for teaching diverse student populations.

Performance Tasks

1. After three weeks of instructional observation, list the observable techniques the teacher uses to either encourage or discourage racism, stereotyping, and sexism.

2. Observe the overall climate of a selected classroom. Identify what techniques the teacher uses to foster a desirable classroom climate.

3. Suggest a minimum of two additional techniques that may improve the classroom climate or discourage racism, stereotyping, or sexism in the classroom under observation.

DATE COMPLETED_____ SUPERVISOR'S SIGNATURE_____

Notes

CHAPTER THREE
MANAGEMENT

Management Competencies

Upon certification, the teacher candidate will have demonstrated the knowledge, skills, attitudes, and judgment necessary to:

1. Identify and implement systems that produce desired changes in student behavior.
2. Design and define operating responsibilities for both the learner and teacher.
3. Provide acceptable physical management of the learning environment.
4. Establish and utilize regular procedures for the acquisition, safe use, storage, and maintenance of equipment, supplies, and other materials.
5. Appropriately supervise noninstructional activities.
6. Prepare appropriate records and reports.

Classroom Management

Performance Objective

After completing three weeks of public school classroom observation, the TC should be able to identify and describe effective and noneffective procedures for classroom management.

Performance Tasks

1. Observe a minimum of three teaching-learning situations. Identify the student control or classroom management problems you have observed.

2. Describe how each of the identified problems was handled by the teacher.

3. What alternative or additional teacher actions, if any, may have been as effective or more effective in handling the identified problems?

4. Identify and explain how some or all of the identified problems may have been avoided.

Continued

DATE COMPLETED_____ SUPERVISOR'S SIGNATURE_____

5. Describe a classroom atmosphere that is most suitable to problem-free operation and facilitates the development of happier and healthier students and teachers.

Notes

Rules and Regulations

Performance Objective

After completing three weeks of public school classroom observation, the TC should be able to identify and explain all-school policies and procedures, as well as any rules and regulations that are specific to the classroom.

Performance Tasks

1. Obtain a copy of the school's student handbook or other similar document. Identify the types of rules and regulations that pertain to students.

2. Talk with a teacher and record the individual classroom rules and regulations that he or she establishes.

3. Observe students in various sections of the school. Do you witness any violations of the school's student rules and regulations? If so, identify them.

4. Observe students in the classroom of the teacher who provided you with his or her individual classroom rules and regulations. Do you witness any violations? If so, identify them.

Continued

DATE COMPLETED_____ SUPERVISOR'S SIGNATURE_____

5. Construct a list of the classroom rules and regulations that you feel would help maintain an orderly and pleasant classroom.

Notes

Student Health and Safety

Performance Objective

After completing three weeks of public school classroom observation, the TC should be able to identify and describe common policies and procedures concerning student health and safety.

Performance Tasks

1. Consult available school documents to identify school policies regarding student health and safety.

2. Ask several teachers about sickness or accidents that have occurred in their classrooms. Identify the health or safety problems involved and how the teacher reacted to the situation.

3. Based on your observations, identify those safety regulations you feel should be in effect in a classroom. Defend your choices.

Notes

Clerical Tasks

Performance Objective

After completing one week of public school classroom observation, the TC should be able to identify common clerical
tasks performed by teachers and describe how these tasks may
be completed effectively.

Performance Tasks

1. Observe a teacher at the very beginning of the school day and
into the first instructional activity. Prepare a list of the clerical
(noninstructional) duties he or she performs.

2. Explain how each of the duties you observed was performed.

3. Interview at least two experienced teachers about the types of
clerical duties they perform. Prepare a list of before-school,
during-school, after-school, and even out-of-school clerical
duties.

DATE COMPLETED_____   SUPERVISOR'S SIGNATURE_____

Notes

The Laboratory

Performance Objective

After completing six weeks of public school laboratory-type observation, the TC should be able to describe a suitable laboratory floorplan and laboratory instructional procedures for a given content area.

Performance Tasks

1. Describe and illustrate the laboratory floorplan, including the location of equipment in the activities you are observing.

2. Identify the content area being taught and describe the laboratory instructional procedures utilized by the teacher.

3. Describe and illustrate an alternative floorplan from the one observed that may be suitable to an effective laboratory activity.

4. Indicate the apparent effectiveness of the instructional procedures observed. Suggest alternative procedures that may also facilitate the laboratory activity.

Notes

Physical Environment

Performance Objective

After completing six weeks of public school classroom observation, the TC should be able to identify desirable qualities of the physical classroom and describe how these qualities may be achieved and maintained.

Performance Tasks

1. Describe the physical environment of the classroom you are observing. Include such things as heat, light, ventilation, space, desks, location of chalkboards, and the like.

2. Prepare a list of environmental facilities or practices that appear to be inadequate. Indicate your reasons.

3. Describe how the physical environment of the classroom could be improved. Recommend changes, additions, or alleviations that may create a more effective learning climate.

DATE COMPLETED_____   SUPERVISOR'S SIGNATURE_____

Notes

Supplies

Performance Objective

After completing six weeks of public school classroom observation, the TC should be able to identify and describe consumable supplies desirable for a given instructional program.

Performance Tasks

1. Prepare a list of the nonreusable supplies the school you are observing furnishes for students. Indicate how students utilize these supplies.

2. Estimate how much of each supply is used by the classroom in one year. Describe any additional supplies that would benefit the instructional program.

3. List any teacher-produced supplies you have observed, such as assignment sheets, programmed materials, learning centers, learning packets, worksheets, and the like.

DATE COMPLETED_____ SUPERVISOR'S SIGNATURE_____

Notes

Equipment

Performance Objective

After completing six weeks of pubic school classroom observation, the TC should be able to list common types of
equipment and materials—as well as their desirable condition,
location, and arrangement—for a given instructional program.

Performance Tasks

1. Prepare a list of all the equipment and nonconsumable supplies in the classroom observed.

2. Illustrate the location, arrangement, and condition of the
equipment and nonconsumable supplies in the classroom.

3. Suggest improvements for the acquisition, safe use, storage,
and maintenance of the classroom's equipment and nonconsumable supplies.

4. Prepare a plan or list of procedures concerning the acquisition,
safe use, storage, and maintenance of equipment, supplies, and
other materials.

DATE COMPLETED_____   SUPERVISOR'S SIGNATURE_____

Notes

The Physical Plant

Performance Objective

After completing six weeks of public school observation, the TC should be able to describe the types, location, and purposes of the physical facilities of a given school.

Performance Tasks

1. Tour the facility in which you are observing. Prepare an illustration of the school's floorplan, indicating locations of classrooms, gym, offices, and so on.

2. Describe what can be seen in each of the following areas at the time you are observing it: cafeteria, gym, main office, auditorium, study hall, hallway, and teachers' lounge.

3. Indicate the main purpose of each of the areas observed.

DATE COMPLETED_____   SUPERVISOR'S SIGNATURE_____

Notes

Teacher Concerns

Performance Objective

After completing six weeks of public school classroom observation, the TC should be able to identify and describe common teacher problems and recommend alternative solutions to them.

Performance Tasks

1. After observing and talking to as many teachers as possible, prepare a list of general teacher problems and concerns. Identify the teachers' two most pronounced concerns.

2. Discuss possible causes for each of the problems or concerns identified.

3. Suggest procedures for alleviating each of the identified problems or concerns.

4. Consider all the teachers you have observed. What percentage seem to apparently tolerate their job but actually dislike it? What teaching duties appear to be tolerable but not desirable? Which ones are intolerable?

DATE COMPLETED_____   SUPERVISOR'S SIGNATURE_____

Notes

LEARNING ACTIVITY CHECKSHEET

Directions: Check (✓) each learning activity completed.

☐ F-1	☐ I-1	☐ M-1
☐ F-2	☐ I-2	☐ M-2
☐ F-3	☐ I-3	☐ M-3
☐ F-4	☐ I-4	☐ M-4
☐ F-5	☐ I-5	☐ M-5
☐ F-6	☐ I-6	☐ M-6
☐ F-7	☐ I-7	☐ M-7
☐ F-8	☐ I-8	☐ M-8
☐ F-9	☐ I-9	☐ M-9
☐ F-10	☐ I-10	☐ M-10
☐ F-11	☐ I-11	
☐ F-12	☐ I-12	
☐ F-13	☐ I-13	
☐ F-14	☐ I-14	
☐ F-15	☐ I-15	
☐ F-16	☐ I-16	
☐ F-17	☐ I-17	
☐ F-18	☐ I-18	
☐ F-19	☐ I-19	
☐ F-20	☐ I-20	
☐ F-21	☐ I-21	
☐ F-22	☐ I-22	

PART THREE

DECISION
ACTIVITIES

To determine your potential success and happiness as a teacher, you must actually experience these things. One method of gaining this experience is through a process of decision activities, which give you the opportunity to feel and participate in educational states of affairs. The decision method also offers you the chance to gain both broad and specific experiences related to the career of teaching.

The activities in this section will give you the opportunity to examine, analyze, evaluate, and formulate individual and group conclusions concerning educational issues in the areas of critical comments, educational dilemmas, professional decision making, and career awareness. Some of the activities described in these four categories are to be completed individually, while others call for large- or small-group discussion and role-playing.

Activities in the first section, **Critical Comments**, present common criticisms of various educational practices. To complete these activities, you must respond to the given criticisms in personal and social ways, identifying the various relevant points of view.

Activities in the **Educational Dilemmas** section deal with contemporary issues in education. To complete these activities, you must identify personal values and philosophical positions about given issues. The emphasis here is on approaching educational issues in a direct and comprehensive manner.

Professional Decision Making activities ask you to react to the day-to-day professional concerns of teachers and administrators. It is important that you maintain a broad perspective while completing each decision-making activity.

In the last section of activities, **Career Awareness**, you will be guided to approach teaching as a career from an organized and planned perspective. These activities will pose the problems and decisions that you will face as a beginning teacher.

CHAPTER FOUR

CRITICAL COMMENTS

Teacher Salaries

Directions

You are a career teacher with 12 years of experience, earning approximately the average salary in your school district. While reading the newspaper, you come across the following letter to the Editor. Write your own letter to the Editor in response to the following:

Editor:

About raising taxes to increase teacher salaries: Taxes are taxes, no matter what they are used for, and there is no way the people of this community can afford an increase. It's about time that teachers realize they are public servants and therefore are employees of the state. This state, as representative of its people, is made up mostly of industrial factory workers. The average salary for teachers in this state, as quoted by a recent copy of the state teachers journal, is $19,322 a year. The average salary of factory workers in this state is $15,000 a year. Isn't this a bit ridiculous? Now teachers, if you ran a business, would you want to pay your help more than you get paid? It's about time education attempts to operate like business, in an efficient and more productive manner.

Concerned Taxpayer

Notes

Teacher Militancy

SMALL-GROUP
ACTIVITY

Directions

You are a teacher in a school system where increased teacher militancy is becoming evident. As part of an in-service program, the following comments were made by a guest speaker from the local Chamber of Commerce. Form groups of 4-5 each and prepare statements of response to these comments that will be submitted to your school system administration and to the Chamber of Commerce. Each statement should represent the viewpoint of each group. Compare statements.

COMMENTS: Teachers have no place in contract negotiations and strikes. . . . As professionals, teachers have no place being militant. . . . Other professionals don't strike. Can you imagine a doctor or lawyer going on strike? . . . Teachers are not factory workers and therefore should not act like them. . . . You must think of the child and your mission.

Notes

School Financial Support

Introduction

The cost of education in the United States is financed mainly through local property taxes. In a 1973 Supreme Court decision, this method of financial support was held to be constitutional in California. However, many argue that this type of educational support does not provide equality of educational opportunity: the wealthier the community, the more taxes collected, the more money spent on education, and, therefore, the better the community, the more money spent on education, and, therefore, the better the education.

Directions

Divide into three groups. Pretend that you are attending a state public hearing concerning the use of property taxes as the basis for school support. Debate the issue from the following points of view:

Group I   Representing citizens in School District I
           Suburban, high-income community
           40 large factories
           $2,500 per pupil expended last year

Group II   Representing citizens in School District II
           Small, bedroom-type community, mostly middle-
                  income residents
           Limited industry
           $1,300 per pupil expended last year

Continued

Group III   Representing citizens in School District III
            Urban, low-income community, large welfare pop-
                ulation
            No industry
            $900 per pupil expended last year

Report individual group views (reflecting small-group consensus) to the total group.

Notes

Equality in Education

Directions

You are a happy, confident, and successful teacher with five years of experience. Today, a new student was assigned to your class. The student's mother brought the child into your classroom during class and, in front of the rest of the students, made the comments below. Because of the circumstances, you told the parent that you would respond to her comments tonight. Prepare a statement in response to the mother's remarks and manner.

COMMENT: My child has had an excellent education in another state. Realizing that education is not as good in this state, I am quite concerned. Therefore, I am requesting that you provide me with a curriculum guide and periodically inform me of what you are doing. I realize that you don't make much money, but it's my right to know what you are doing to my child. I'll be dropping in from time to time to observe you.

Notes

Teaching: "A Gravy Train"

Introduction

Critics of teachers and education have always been quick to comment that teaching is an easy source of money. It is readily assumed that teachers are overpaid for what they do.

Directions

Form groups of 4–5 each. Discuss the following comments and prepare a reaction to them. Compare the reactions among groups.

COMMENTS: Some school systems pay teachers over a 12-month period when they only teach for 9 months. . . . Three-month paid vacation, all the holiday vacations, and 8–3 hours—a real gravy train. . . . Anyone can sit with kids for a few hours a day—terribly high babysitting rates to pay teachers.

Notes

Accountability

Introduction

Many business executives have criticized educators for not controlling education as efficiently as business and industry have been controlled. For instance, automobile industry executives have commented that if they could not guarantee their product any better than educators can, they would be out of business. The validity of such guarantees has been tested in state courts over recent years, where students have charged school systems with not providing acceptable learning. Few teachers, however, have been released from their positions because students have failed to learn. Nonetheless, accountability is becoming an increasing reality in education.

Directions

Prepare a one-page position paper concerning accountability in education, reflecting your views on the statements above. Support your position.

Notes

Teaching: "A Good Job for a Woman"

Directions

Form all-male and all-female groups of 4–5 each. Discuss the following comments and prepare a group statement in reaction. Compare statements among groups and debate the different reactions.

COMMENTS: Teaching is an excellent job for a woman. What other job permits a woman to be off from work at all of the times that her children are off from school? Also, with summer and holiday vacations, it's a part-time job for a full-time salary. And there's no discrimination; women are paid on the same basis as men. But most women teachers aren't breadwinners; they just provide a second income for their families. They might be married to someone who earns $70,000 a year. Now compare that to a male teacher who earns $18,000 and has to support a wife and seven children. People with such different lifestyles have to have different values. As teachers, how could they agree on anything?

Notes

"If Nothing Else—Teach"

Directions

Answer the following questions as honestly as you can:

1. List three career qualities that are important to you. Consider your personal and professional life.

2. List five careers that you may like to pursue.

3. How does teaching rank on your list?

4. What do you see yourself doing 10 years from now?

5. Would a career in education be compatible with your likes and dislikes, both personal and professional? Explain.

Notes

Teaching: "Love It or Leave It"

Directions

Pretend that you are a third-year teacher, discussing salary and fringe benefits, as well as school finance and teacher militancy in general, with a small group of colleagues in the teachers' lounge. While you are talking, another colleague enters the room, listens for a minute, and makes the comment below. Prepare a brief statement in reaction to the comment. Do not sign your name. Collect and redistribute the papers, allowing each person to read aloud the reaction on the paper he or she receives. Compare and discuss the reactions.

COMMENT: Teachers are all getting alike. I'm sick of always hearing about not enough money. You people knew you wouldn't earn much money teaching. If you don't like it, get out of the business.

Notes

Criticism Continuum

Directions

Make an **X** at the point on the continuum that best represents your feelings on the following:

1. Teacher salaries are currently:

Too low	About right	Too high

2. Teachers in today's schools are:

Too militant	About right	Not militant enough

3. Schools should be financed by:

Property taxes	Combination	Income taxes

4. Teacher-training institutions should:

Extremely limit the number of teacher graduates	In no way limit the number of teacher graduates

5. The quality of education in this country:

Varies extremely from state to state	Does not differ from state to state

6. Compared to other careers, teaching is:

A difficult job for the money	About average	An easy job for the money

7. In the United States, public schools are normally:

In no way accountable	About average	Extremely accountable

Continued

8. Women in education, by the very nature of their employment circumstances, are:

Detrimental to education as a profession	No different than men	Very beneficial to education as a profession

9. Comparing the advantages with the disadvantages of teaching, what is your interest in teaching as a career?

Disadvantages make it undesirable	Undecided	Advantages make it desirable

10. The future rewards of teaching, financial and/or otherwise, appear personally to be:

Extremely beneficial	Average	Extremely unsatisfactory

Record all participants' responses on a single list. Compare your responses with the compilation.

Notes

CHAPTER FIVE

EDUCATIONAL DILEMMAS

Introduction

A *dilemma* can be defined as a situation requiring a choice between two or more equally unsatisfactory alternatives. Public school personnel—especially administrators—are quite often faced with educational dilemmas. To become familiar with the tasks of facing a dilemma, complete the following exercise. The consequences of this dilemma are tragic, making this one of the most difficult dilemmas anyone can face.

DILEMMA: You are traveling with your spouse and child aboard an airplane flying at 37,000 feet. A bomb explodes and you are notified that the plane will crash. You are given a parachute and instructed how and where to deplane. You are told that you can only take one member of your family with you; the other will have to crash with the plane. In short, you can save one person and the other will definitely be killed. Who would you save?

Directions

Keep your decision to yourself. Discuss the dilemma and its application to educational decision making.

Notes

The Busing Problem

SMALL-GROUP ACTIVITY **ED-2**

Introduction

Busing students to achieve racial desegregation has become an extreme problem for public schools ever since the 1971 U.S. Supreme Court ruled that it was mandatory. Public school officials continue to experience extreme anxiety over the busing dilemma. In addition to the issue of whether or not to comply, officials must face the alternative approaches to busing, the effects of busing on students, and the pressures applied by local interest groups for and against busing.

DILEMMA: You are a teacher in a school system that must implement a plan for school desegregation for next fall. Your school superintendent has appointed you to one of several study groups being formed to recommend such a plan.

Directions

Form groups of 4–5 each. Discuss alternative plans for desegregating the public school system and prepare a recommendation. Reach the decision for the recommendation by group consensus. Do not vote. Compare and defend the different groups' recommendations.

Notes

To Track?

Introduction

Tracking—grouping students with similar characteristics into common classes—has become a most frequent occurrence in today's public schools. It is not uncommon to find three classes of students for most subject areas. English 7, for example, may have Track A, for the above-average student; Track B, for the average student; and Track C, for the below-average student. All three tracks of students will be taught essentially the same subject matter but at different difficulty levels and in different ways.

DILEMMA: You are a teacher in a school system that is faced with developing a policy statement on student tracking. Your school superintendent has received criticism, both supportive and nonsupportive, of student tracking and must implement a school system policy for its use.

Directions

Form groups of 4–5 each. First, each group should develop a list of the advantages and disadvantages of tracking. Second, each group should develop a policy statement concerning tracking, including supportive reasons for the decision.

Notes

The Parochial Controversy

Introduction

The use of tax money to support private and parochial schools has long been an issue reaching state and federal courts. The advantages and disadvantages offered regarding the parochiad controversy are highly dependent on the personal backgrounds and beliefs of the individuals perceiving the issue. Thus, the issue remains controversial.

DILEMMA: The State Department of Education is holding hearings concerning tax support of private and parochial schools in an attempt to formulate a state parochiad policy. The state has invited various interest groups to the hearing to present their views, including (1) the Association of Private Schools; (2) the John Birch Society; (3) the Christian Education Association; and (4) the Association of Concerned Public School Parents.

Directions

Form four groups, one representing each of the associations listed above. Each group should prepare a policy statement representing the perceived feeling of the association and read it aloud to the others. After each of the groups has read its statement, debate the issue from the viewpoint of your representative body.

Notes

Cutting Expenses:
Where and How?

Introduction

School systems throughout the nation are experiencing economic problems of various degrees. Most school systems are implementing various methods of cutting their expenses, including releasing faculty, freezing salaries, reducing administrative staff, cutting maintenance, and enlarging class sizes.

DILEMMA: Your superintendent of schools has recently become aware that his operating budget for next year will be cut by 20 percent, which means he must develop a plan for cutting operating expenses by the same amount. To help him do so, the superintendent has appointed various committees of teachers to make recommendations for cutting expenses. You have been assigned to one of these committees.

Directions

Form groups of 4–5 each. Each group should prepare a list, in order of priority, of the recommended methods for cutting expenses. Compare and discuss the recommendations proposed by the various groups.

Notes

Sex Education:
Whose Responsibility?

Introduction

Sex education has been a controversial issue faced by public
school officials over the past several decades. Decisions must
often be made concerning the inclusion of sex education in the
curriculum: as part of what subject should it be taught, in what
manner, by whom, and under whose direction?

DILEMMA: You are a member of a local school board addressing
a hotly debated issue: sex education. You must vote for or
against sex education in your school system and defend your
decision to members of the press. Other members of the board
are evenly split, for and against, so your vote is the deciding
factor.

Directions

Prepare a statement to be released to the press, indicating your
decision concerning sex education in the curriculum and the
reasons for your choice.

Notes

Censorship vs. Academic Freedom

Introduction

Periodically, controversies arise concerning the textbooks used in the public schools. Often, the controversy comes from citizens protesting the use of books that contain supposedly obscene, pornographic, anti-American or antireligious writings. Public school officials are often faced with arguments equally supportive and nonsupportive of such protestors' concerns.

DILEMMA: After receiving a number of parent complaints regarding the use of several textbooks, the superintendent of your school system has asked you to prepare a policy statement concerning controversial textbooks.

Directions

Prepare a specific policy that could be utilized to determine the acceptability of textbooks. Include administrative procedures and persons involved in policy implementation.

Notes

LEARNING ACTIVITY ED-7
Censorship vs. Academic Freedom

170

Contract Negotiations

Introduction

Contract negotiations have become commonplace in education over recent years. School boards are faced with unsurmountable financial problems, while teachers increasingly demand higher salaries and economic benefits. Reaching an agreement in contract negotiations is difficult for both school boards and teachers, often posing a true dilemma.

DILEMMA: Negotiations between the school board and teachers have been going on for 12 weeks. An impasse has become inevitable, unless one side is willing to negotiate further.

Directions

Divide into two groups, one representative of the school board and one representative of the teachers. Each group should select 3-4 representatives for collective bargaining. As a group, prepare a brief list of demands (teachers) or offerings (school board) in the areas of salary, fringe benefits, working conditions, and miscellaneous. Within one class period, the representatives should negotiate what they have prepared. An agreement must be reached by the end of the given period.

Notes

Increasing Taxes

Introduction

The financial crisis in many school systems has increased dramatically in recent years. Faced with substantial increases in maintaining facilities and often decreasing tax support, public school officials find themselves in a dilemma. Tax increases have never been a popular solution to this problem. Yet, as a tax-supported agency, the school system relies on this source for total support. When school system needs exceed financial resources, a most difficult decision must be made.

DILEMMA: You are a teacher in a school system that has experienced an increase in student enrollment. The present facilities are not large enough to handle all the students and they are badly in need of repair. To raise money to build a new facility would require a tax increase. To raise money to repair the old facilities could possibly be accommodated by cutting expenses in other areas. As a teacher representative of your school, you must recommend to the superintendent the course of action she should take. You may recommend the construction of a new facility, the repairing of the old facility, or leaving the facilities as they are and just making do.

Directions

Form groups of 4–5 each. Each group should prepare a group recommendation of what action to take, offering supportive reasons. Compare and discuss the recommendations of the various groups.

Notes

Dilemma Continuum

Directions

Make an **X** at the point on each continuum that best represents your feelings on the following:

1. Busing students for racial desegregation:

Should never be permitted	Should be permitted in some cases	Should always be permitted

2. Tracking students:

Should never be permitted	Should be permitted in some cases	Should always be permitted

3. Providing tax money to support private and parochial schools:

Should never be permitted	Should be permitted in some cases	Should always be permitted

4. The place of sex education is:

In the school	In the school and the home	In the home

5. Textbook selection should be the responsibility of:

Teachers	Teachers and parents	Parents

6. Prayer in school:

Should never be allowed	Should sometimes be allowed	Should be required

7. Students lockers should be searched:

Never	Periodically	Routinely

Record all participants' responses on a single list. Compare your responses with the compilation.

Notes

CHAPTER SIX

PROFESSIONAL DECISION MAKING

Selecting Techniques

Introduction

Throughout your education, you were exposed to various forms of teaching techniques, including lectures, discussions, panels, individual assignments, and demonstrations. Some of these techniques worked for some teachers but failed for others. And some of these techniques worked for some classes but not others.

Directions

Specify the type(s) of teaching technique(s) that would most likely be effective for you and the following classes of learners in the subject and/or grade level of your choice. Indicate how you would implement the technique(s).

Class 1   A group of 38 students of all ability levels with no apparent common interests; categorized as an average group.

Class 2   A group of 30 students of low academic ability; most lack motivation and interest in the subject and in school, in general.

Class 3   A group of 15 high-academic ability students; extremely motivated and responsible.

Class 4   A group of 25 students, all of about average ability; some are motivated, some are not.

Notes

Problem Situations

Directions

Consider each of the following problem situations and decide how you would react given the circumstances.

Situation 1

You are in the middle of teaching a lesson that appears to be going quite well when two students become violently angry at one another and begin fighting in the classroom. They both outweigh you by at least 20 pounds. What would you do?

Situation 2

It is near the end of a long, tiring day and your habitual problem student makes you very angry. In a moment of anger, you shout, "Get out of here. And I never want to see you again!" The student stares you in the eye and says, "Make me." What would you do?

Situation 3

During one of your classes, one student accuses another of tearing up his important assignment. The accused student violently denies it and no one else saw what happened. Both students need the issue to be settled immediately. What would you do?

Continued

Situation 4

Late at night, you receive a phone call from one of your student's irrate parents. He accuses you of dehumanizing and disgracing his daughter and says that he will be at school early in the morning, waiting to settle things with you. What would you do?

Situation 5

One of your students has been in trouble with the law and has confided in you over the past three weeks. You have been trying to help her solve her problems and she trusts you. The police come to talk to you in an attempt to get information. You know that by talking to the police, the student may be helped. And the police inform you that you may be obstructing the law by not talking. Nonetheless, the student has placed her trust in you and is depending on you not to talk. What would you do?

Notes

The Teachers' Lounge

Directions

Consider each of the following problem situations and decide how you would react given the cirumstances.

Situation 1

You walk into the teachers' lounge rather suddenly and catch a fellow faculty member taking a drink of gin. You have heard talk about his drinking and have indications that his students have been suffering from his poor teaching. However, he is your department head and tells you that the outcome of your yearly evaluation depends on your keeping quiet. What would you do?

Situation 2

Each day in the teachers' lounge, you listen to a group of teachers ridicule a particular student. You also know the student, but, in addition, you know of his peculiar personal problems. The other teachers are unaware of the student's underlying problems and appear to be causing him undue hardship in their classes. The teachers are quite insecure and defensive and don't appear to take criticism well themselves. You want their friendship but also have real concern for the student. What would you do?

Situation 3

While relaxing in the lounge, you overhear a group of teachers planning a practical joke on a beginning teacher. The joke being planned would embarrass the teacher in front of his students. You know that the beginning teacher has been experiencing difficulty and is contemplating quitting his job.

Continued

But he is a good teacher and, with time, could most likely become an excellent teacher. You, too, are a beginning teacher and will probably jeopardize your chance for friendship with the group if you do anything about what you hear. What would you do?

Notes

Student Evaluation

Directions

Make an **X** at the point of the continuum that best represents your feelings on the following issue. Discuss your choice.

Students should be graded on:

Effort	A combination of effort and competency	Competency

Consider each of the following situations and decide how you would react given the circumstances.

Situation 1

You have given your first big test as a beginning teacher. Your students have been told that they will receive an A for 93–100 points, a B for 86–92 points, a C for 78–85 points, a D for 70–77 points, and an F for below 70 points. This test is to be worth 50 percent of their report card grade. After correcting the papers, you find that the highest score is a 68. What would you do?

Situation 2

You are teaching two groups of students the same subject matter. One group is of high-academic students, and the other is of low-academic students. At the end of a report card period, no one in the low-academic group knows as much as the poorest student in the high-academic group. How would you determine report cards for the two groups?

Notes

Controversial Issues

Directions

Form groups of 4–5 each and prepare a reaction statement to the following quotations. Compare and discuss the reactions among groups.

Quotation 1

"Teachers should remain absolutely neutral in all matters dealing with controversial issues."

Quotation 2

"Teachers should attempt to teach acceptable values to all students in all classes."

Quotation 3

"Teachers should teach only that which is compatible to the norms of the community in which the school is located."

Quotation 4

"Teachers should integrate common religious beliefs into all classes."

Quotation 5

"Teachers should find time to discuss any and all controversial issues that are of interest to students."

Notes

Crisis Situations

Directions

Form groups of 4–5 each. Discuss the following crisis situations and, as a group, recommend a desirable course of action for each. Compare and discuss the recommendations among groups.

Situation 1

You are the principal of a large, modern school. The police have informed you that they suspect drug violations are occurring in your school and desire to place several undercover officers in the building. After careful consideration, you refuse and they agree to disband their plan. Later, you learn that they have implemented their plan, despite your objections. Students find out and storm your office. What would you do?

Situation 2

You are the principal of a large, modern high school. Shortly before the end of the lunch period, fighting breaks out between small groups of black and white students. You must decide whether to attempt to stop the fight before it increases, to just stay out of it and call the police, or to take other measures. What would you do?

Situation 3

You are the only counselor in a school of about 400 students. You become so involved with administrative tasks that you find little time for counseling duties. Students have protested and teachers have complained that you are not providing them with the proper support. And this morning, the principal entered your office with a list of faculty signatures requesting your dismissal. What would you do?

Continued

Situation 4

You are a teacher in a large, modern high school. As you are passing through the hall, you observe a drug transaction between two students, one of whom is a star athlete and the other, a student believed responsible for a good deal of the drug traffic in the school. The two students know that you have seen them. You have specific orders to report any such incidents. You feel threatened by the drug-dealing student but feel a responsibility for stopping the traffic. Yet you feel sorry for the athlete and know that by reporting the incident, you may jeopardize a brilliant future. What would you do?

Notes

Teacher Evaluation

Introduction

Faculty evaluation is an extremely difficult but necessary responsibility of school principals. Some principals handle the evaluation entirely by themselves; others use department heads and/or other faculty members to aid in the evaluation process. Evaluation procedures usually include classroom visitations and interviews; in some cases, student evaluations of teachers may also be used.

Directions

Form groups of 4–5 each. Each group should devise a comprehensive method or process of teacher evaluation, including a list of the items by which each teacher should be evaluated. Compare and discuss the outcomes among the various groups.

Notes

Teacher Dismissal

Directions

Form groups of 4-5 each. As a group, recommend a course of action for each of the following situations. Reach group decisions by consensus. Do not vote.

Situation 1

You are a principal in a school with 60 teachers. You have been receiving various anonymous messages accusing two of your teachers of engaging in immoral activities within the school. The male teacher involved is married and the female is not. After some investigation, you find several students who admit to observing the activity. What would you do?

Situation 2

You are the principal of a small, rural school with 300 students. You have received various reports concerning the suspected homosexuality of one of your teachers. What would you do?

Situation 3

As principal of a school with 35 teachers, you have observed that one teacher appears to be incompetent. You base your observation on student complaints, as well as consistently low student test scores on standardized tests. What would you do?

Continued

Situation 4

You are the superintendent of schools in a community of about 30,000 people. You have received numerous complaints from parents concerning one of your principals. Namely, the complaints state that the principal is too lax in discipline and runs a wide-open, uncontrolled school. After various visits to the school, you perceive that students are actively involved in learning. By talking to teachers in the school, you find that they are split in their opinions of the principal. The school board has requested your recommendation concerning dismissal. What would you do?

Notes

CHAPTER SEVEN

CAREER
AWARENESS

"The Teacher Is . . ."

Introduction

A teacher means something different to each of us and many things to many people. Each of our perception of teachers is derived from experiences, good and bad, accumulated over our years of schooling. As 12- to 13-year participants in various types of schools, we are all experts in education (or at least we think we are). Nonetheless, having experienced learning under the direction of several teachers, each of us does have personal feelings concerning effective and ineffective teachers.

Directions

1. List all the teachers you can remember having in your elementary and high school years.

2. List one thing that you remember best about each one.

3. Indicate which teachers you think were the most effective and which were the least effective, supporting your evaluation.

4. Describe your perception of the ideal teacher.

5. Describe how you see yourself as a teacher in 10 years.

6. Prepare a personal résumé advertising yourself for a teaching position now. Prepare another as if it were 10 years from now.

Notes

Job Selection

Introduction

Deciding on your first teaching position is an important decision. Although the number of available jobs may be limited, potential teachers can make strategic decisions concerning where and how they look for a teaching position. The following questions may prove helpful.

1. What is the proximity of the school to a college or university at which you could work on an advanced degree?
2. What duties would the position involve? Would you be teaching in your major and/or minor teaching field and/or helping in cocurricular activities? Also, how many classes would you teach, with how many students in each?
3. Will you be properly certified?
4. Do the salary schedule and fringe benefits satisfy you?
5. With whom would you be working—teachers, administrators, and students?
6. How far do you want to be from home?
7. What chances for advancement would you have with the school and/or school system?

Directions

You are a graduate of a teacher-training institution and certified to teach in your state. Prepare a description of what you consider to be the ideal teaching position. Utilize the questions above, as well as any other information that may be important to you.

Notes

Advanced Degrees

Introduction

One of the advantages a career in teaching offers is the opportunity to pursue advanced degrees. Teachers often have the chance to work on advanced degrees in the summer and at night during the regular school year. Moreover, a wide range of possibilities for degree preparation is usually available. According to an individual's goals and interests, a teacher may choose to pursue a master's degree in an academic area (such as English, science, math, and so on) or in an area of education (including elementary education, secondary education, educational administration, counselor education, special education, educational foundations, vocational education, and so forth).

Directions

You are a beginning teacher and are seriously considering whether or not to pursue a master's degree. Prepare a list of the factors that you must consider in making your decision. Secondly, make your decision and explain why you made it.

Notes

Career Planning

Introduction

Where do you want to be and what do you want to be doing 10 years from now? Future success may be dependent on early and careful planning. Identifying goals and a course of action to attain these goals may alleviate many future hours of confusion and indecision.

Directions

1. Describe how you would like to be 10 years from now. Include aspects of both your professional and personal life.

2. Identify in sequence everything you need to do in order to reach these goals.

3. Identify your strengths and weaknesses that may aid or hinder you in these plans.

4. Outline two or more career plans of jobs in which you are interested. Indicate the one or ones in which you are the most interested.

5. What do you think you will be doing 10 years from now if you do not follow through with any of these plans?

Notes

Teaching as Tolerating

Directions

You are a teacher with three years of experience. The teacher in the classroom next to you has submitted the following personal statement to the local teachers' organization for distribution to all teachers in the system. Based on this statement, prepare a description of the teacher as you would perceive him or her. Include personal and professional concerns and backgrounds, as well as classroom performance.

My Fellow Teachers:

In an age of social unrest, today's public schools have become common markets for the exchange of all the social ills affecting modern society. As the public school teacher stumbles helplessly in an attempt to treat the troubled and diseased youth, he finds that he is operating under the surveillance of various right- and left-wing organizations, civil liberty groups, and numerous community and parental interest groups. As the operation of the teacher's tasks progresses confusingly toward the goals of educating today's youth and cleansing the diseased society, the role of the teacher has become less one of educating and more one of tolerating.

For somewhat less than obvious reasons, the public schools have been selected as the social agency to cure American society of racism, anti-Americanism, apathy, moral degradation, poverty, and whatever else any particular group finds wrong. The teacher, as a practitioner or craftsman, tolerates the demands of his employer—the public—and un-convincingly sets out to perform something not short of a miracle in an attempt to reconstruct the social, political, personal, ethical, and intellectual nature of students who have been "corrupted by today's society." But the student refuses to believe that it is he who is corrupt. He reverses the arguments so authoritatively pronounced upon him, and his parents and teachers become the targets for blame and resistance. The teacher, therefore, is found in a most frustrating position,

Continued

where he cannot possibly perform what is required of him. He is caught in a web of public demand, student resistance, and personal beliefs.

Personal beliefs are most often sacrificed. Values and attitudes are, more times than not, displaced. Curricular activities are arranged to meet the demands of students or the public. The schools, in an attempt to control the complex problems bestowed by society, have resorted to permissiveness. Dress codes, personal health requirements, and ethical decency exist only as antiques. The schools are not curing the ills of society by yielding to them. They are not curing the "corrupt society," as defined by the public or the "now generation." They are simply publicizing that the society is diseased and, in a sense, spreading it around. The teacher, as a public servant, finds that his role in this undertaking becomes one of toleration. He often despises what he is doing, but he tolerates it.

Participants of the "now generation" are gradually beginning to appear in the classroom on the teacher's side of the desk. As teachers are pulled between students and the public in a political, social, intellectual, ethical, and highly personal tug of war and find that they are required to sacrifice personal values and attitudes, teacher militancy has become a reality. The "now generation" of teachers are not willing to accept toleration in their job description. But even in the miotic stages of teacher militancy, teachers themselves are the teaching profession's worst enemies.

At no time in the history of mankind has a profession or labor group so large in number been so unorganized, powerless, fragmented, and servitude. Teachers, the largest group of individuals employed in the same profession or semiprofession in the United States, are still unable to get the attention of political leaders, who exert little energy to attract the teacher vote. As an organization and as individuals, teachers continue to tolerate their political, social, and personal image. Until teachers become politically and socially involved, this image will remain substandard with the public and tolerable with teachers.

In today's schools, teaching means **tolerating**; in today's society, as well, teachers are basically tolerators.

Notes

Which Level to Choose?

Introduction

Three or four distinct levels of public school teaching are usually recognized in education. Normally included are the levels of early childhood education, elementary education, intermediate education, and secondary education. If one is interested in teaching, he or she should carefully choose the level at which he or she would be the most effective, as well as the happiest.

Directions

1. Prepare a list of the advantages and disadvantages of teaching at each of the four levels specified above, based on your own experience and observations.
2. Describe yourself 10 years from now in one of the following teaching situations.
   a. You are teaching kindergarten: 25 students in the morning and 25 different students in the afternoon.
   b. You are teaching math and reading to two separate groups of fifth-graders.
   c. You are teaching all subjects to a class of 30 third-graders.
   d. You are teaching five classes, including sixth-, seventh-, and eighth-graders, in a middle school.
   e. You are teaching your major subject of interest in a high school.

Notes

The Private Life of a Teacher

Directions

As a career teacher, how would you respond to the following quotations?

Quotation 1

"Teachers have a responsibility to use absolute discretion in their personal lives."

Quotation 2

"A secondary but extremely important role of a teacher is that of proctor of morality."

Quotation 3

"Teachers are public servants and should never become involved in controversial situations."

Quotation 4

"As public servants, teachers have no place in politics."

Quotation 5

"What a teacher does outside of school is totally up to him or her."

Continued

Quotation 6

"Teachers with any type of questionable moral character have no place in the classroom."

Quotation 7

"Romantic relationships among teachers in the same school should be disallowed."

Notes

To Strike?

Introduction

The legal and moral questions involving teacher strikes have become an increasing concern of public school teachers. And as state legislatures approve collective bargaining legislation, the potential for teacher strikes appears to be increasing.

Directions

Consider the following problem situation and indicate your reaction to the given circumstances.

Situation

You are a successful teacher with 10 years of experience. The collective bargaining deliberations in your school district have reached an impasse. You are called to a meeting of all teachers to vote on a strike, which would begin tomorrow. There are several speeches given before the vote is taken. Several persons stress the reasons for striking, while a few speak out against it. How would you vote in this situation? Consider all personal and professional circumstances. Specify the reasons for your choice.

Notes

14
LH